Heat Wave

Catherine Chambers

Heinemann Library
Chicago, Illinois

Customer Service 888-454-2279

Visit our website at www.heinemannlibrary.com

Designed by Visual Image
Illustration by Paul Bale
Originated by Ambassador Litho
Printed and bound in South China

06 05 04 03 02
10 9 8 7 6 5 4 3 2 1

Library of Congress Cataloging-in-Publication Data
Chambers, Catherine, 1954-
   Heat wave / Catherine Chambers.
       p. cm. -- (Wild weather)
Includes index.
Summary: Describes what causes heat waves, the conditions that exist
during a heat wave, their harmful and beneficial effects, and their
impact on humans, plants, and animals.
   ISBN 1-58810-657-8 (HC), 1-4034-0113-6 (Pbk)
   1. Heat waves (Meteorology)--Juvenile literature. 2.
Heat--Physiological effect--Juvenile literature. [1. Heat waves
(Meteorology)] I. Title. II. Series.
   QC981.8.A5 C5 2002
   551.5'25--dc21
                                   2002000820

Acknowledgments

The author and publishers are grateful to the following for permission to reproduce copyright material: pp. 4, 7, 16, 20,
25, 26 Photodisc; pp. 5, 13, 17, 19, 21, 27 Associated Press; pp. 8, 11, 15, 23, 28 Corbis; p. 9 Robert Harding Picture
Library; pp. 10, 14 Science Photo Library; p. 12 Tudor Photography; p. 18 PA Photos/EPA; p. 22 FLPA; pp. 24, 29
Stone/Getty.

Cover photograph: Corbis.

The publishers would like to thank the Met Office for their assistance with the preparation of this book.

Every effort has been made to contact copyright holders of any material reproduced in this book. Any omissions will be
rectified in subsequent printings if notice is given to the publisher.

Some words are shown in bold, **like this.** You can
find out what they mean by looking in the glossary.

Contents

What Is a Heat Wave?

A heat wave is a long period of very hot weather. In many heat waves there are no clouds to block the Sun's rays and no breezes to cool us down.

A long period of heat can dry up the ground.
Many plants will **wilt** and die. People and
animals can get very hot and thirsty during a
heat wave.

Where Do Heat Waves Happen?

Heat waves can happen almost anywhere. Many happen in the middle of **continents.** Places that are far from large bodies of water do not get as many cooling breezes.

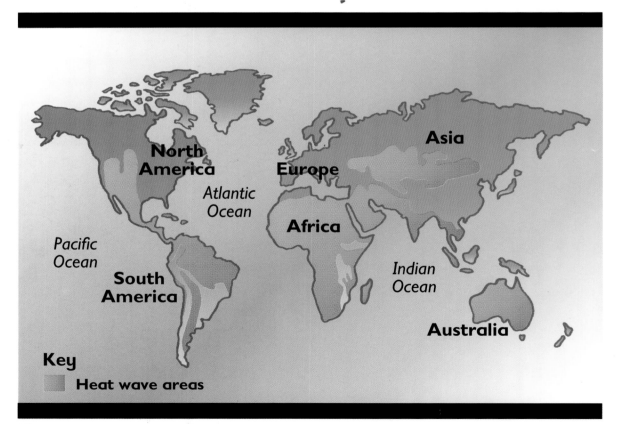

North America

Atlantic Ocean

Europe

Asia

Africa

Pacific Ocean

South America

Indian Ocean

Australia

Key

Heat wave areas

Islands can suffer from heat waves, too. The sea is usually very calm and still when there is a heat wave. There are no winds to cool the land.

Why Is it So Hot?

The weather is usually hotter in the summer. More of the Sun's heat reaches the part of the Earth we live on. Clouds can keep some of this heat from reaching us.

In this picture the sky is clear. There are no clouds to keep the Sun from beating down. There is no breeze to cool the land.

Why Do Heat Waves Happen?

Heat waves happen when **masses** of hot air stay over one place for a long time. These masses are called high **pressure** masses. This weather map shows areas of high and low pressure.

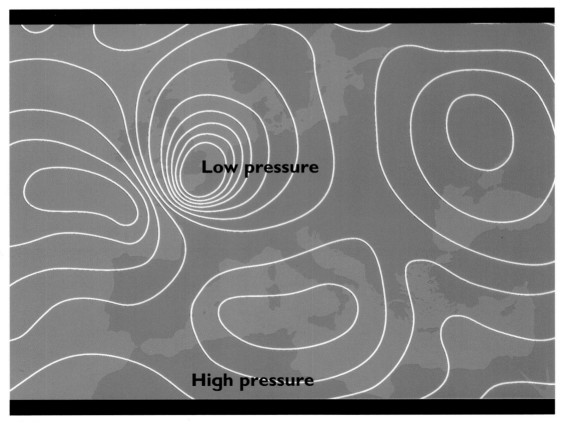

Low pressure

High pressure

Winds blow away from high pressure areas to low pressure areas. A large mass of high pressure can keep winds from blowing in from other places. The air is very still.

What Are Heat Waves Like?

During a heat wave, the **temperature** is very high. This **thermometer** shows a temperature of 110°F (44°C).

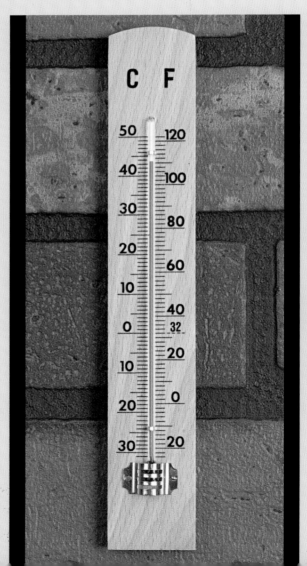

City streets get hot and dusty during a heat wave. The air is still and **hazy** with smelly **fumes.** Sidewalks are too hot to walk on with bare feet.

Harmful Heat Waves

There is very little wind in a heat wave. So **gases** from car engines and factory chimneys do not blow away. Cities get very **polluted.** Some people find it hard to breathe.

Things that are made of metal, like cars, become too hot to touch. When the weather is very hot and sunny, you can often see **mirages** on the roads. They look like puddles of water.

Heat Wave in the City

Chicago, Illinois, is in the middle of a **continent,** so it is often very hot in the summer. It is also near a large lake, which makes it **humid.** When there is a heat wave it gets even hotter.

There was a terrible heat wave in Chicago in 1995. Many people got sick from the heat. Their bodies could not cool themselves down. Some people became very ill.

Preparing for Heat Waves

Weather **forecasters** can predict heat waves by looking at pictures taken by **satellites** far above the Earth. The pictures tell them what kind of weather is moving into their area.

Some people stock up on water and cool drinks
if they know a heat wave is coming. It is very
important to drink enough water when the
weather is hot.

Keeping Cool

People wear lightweight clothes in a heat wave. Sometimes office workers wear shorts instead of suits. Wearing a hat will protect you from the Sun's rays.

The best way of keeping cool is to get wet!
Many people walk through water sprays in
parks or play in sprinklers. A trip to the
swimming pool is a good way to cool down.

21

Coping with Heat Waves

There was a long heat wave in Greece recently. The city became hot and stuffy with **fumes** from cars and factories. People stopped driving their cars to avoid making more fumes.

People tried to shade themselves from the rays of the Sun. You should always protect your skin from sunburn by wearing **sunblock** and a hat.

Animals and Plants in a Heat Wave

When the weather is cold, cats grow extra fur to keep themselves warm. In the summer, they keep cool by shedding the extra fur. Pets need plenty of drinking water in a heat wave.

Plants need water to live and grow. During
a heat wave, they lose water more quickly.
Farmers use sprinklers to make sure their
crops have enough water.

To the Rescue!

Too much heat can make you ill. During a heat wave people often suffer from **heatstroke.** If you start to feel dizzy and sick, you should go to a cool place.

Heat waves can harm farm animals, so they are often herded into the shade. Farm workers bring plenty of drinking water in trucks.

Adapting to Heat Waves

Ceiling fans or air conditioning help to cool down homes, offices, and schools during a heat wave. At home, people often use portable fans that plug into the wall.

In some countries, buildings are designed to
keep out the heat. The walls are very thick.
They are painted white to **reflect** the Sun. The
windows are small and have shutters.

Fact File

◆ During a heat wave the **temperature** can be so high that the tar on roads melts.

◆ When the weather is very **humid,** it often feels hotter than the temperature on a **thermometer.** Scientists have developed a scale called the heat index. It combines the temperature and the humidity to tell you how hot it feels.

◆ The highest temperature ever recorded was in Libya, Africa, on September 13, 1922. It reached 136°F (58°C) that day!

Glossary

continent huge mass of land, such as Africa

crop plant that is grown for food

forecaster someone who predicts what kind of weather we will get

fumes smelly harmful gases

gas light, usually invisible substance. Air contains many different gases.

hazy not clear

heatstroke serious illness caused by heat

humid containing a lot of moisture

mass large amount of something like air that does not have a definite shape

mirage something that you think you see but that is not really there

pollute to spoil with harmful gases or other substances

pressure pushing force

reflect to bounce back

satellite spacecraft that travels around Earth

sunblock lotion that protects your skin from the Sun

temperature measure of how hot or cold it is

thermometer tool that is used for measuring temperature

wilt to get floppy as a result of not having enough water

More Books to Read

Ashwell, Miranda, and Andy Owen. *Sunshine.* Chicago: Heinemann Library, 1999.

Burton, Margie, with Cathy French and Tammy Jones. *Heat.* Pelham, N.Y.: Benchmark Education Company, 1999.

Burke, Jennifer S. *Hot Days.* Danbury, Conn.: Children's Press, 2000.

Index